The INSIDE & OUT GUIDE to
YOUR BODY

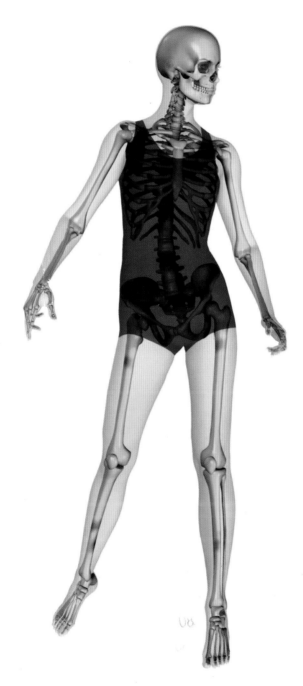

THE INSIDE AND OUT GUIDE TO YOUR BODY
was produced by

David West 👫 **Children's Books**

7 Princeton Court
55 Felsham Road
London SW15 1AZ

Designer: David West
Editor: Dominique Crowley
Picture Research: Victoria Cook

First published in Great Britain by Heinemann
Library, Halley Court, Jordan Hill, Oxford
OX2 8EJ, part of Harcourt Education.
Heinemann is a registered trademark
of Harcourt Education Ltd.

11 10 09 08 07
10 9 8 7 6 5 4 3 2 1

10 digit ISBN: 0 431 18306 6 (hardback)
13 digit ISBN: 978 0 431 18306 0
10 digit ISBN: 0 431 18313 9 (paperback)
13 digit ISBN: 978 0 431 18313 8

British Library Cataloguing in Publication Data

Parker, Steve
    Your body. - (The inside & out guides)
    1. Body, Human - Juvenile literature 2.Human
    physiology - Juvenile literature 3.Human
    anatomy - Juvenile literature
    I. Title
    612

Printed and bound in China

PHOTO CREDITS :
Abbreviations: t-top, m-middle, b-bottom, r-right,
l-left, c-centre.

7br, Bone marrow – Prof. P. Motta/Dept. of
Anatomy/Univeristy "La Sapienza", Rome/Science
Photo Library; 11tr, Jamie West; 16b, Rob Gentile;
18b, Vocal cords open – CNRI/Science Photo Library,
Vocal cords closed – CNRI/Science Photo Library;
22t, Blood clot – Steve Gschmeissner/Science Photo
Library; 22br, White cell attacking bacteria – Eye of
Science/ Science Photo Library; 26t, Inside nose –
Anatomical Travelogue/ Science Photo Library; 26b,
Taste buds – Omikron/ Science Photo Library

Every effort has been made to contact copyright
holders of any material reproduced in this book.
Any omissions will be rectified in subsequent
printings if notice is given to the publishers.

*An explanation of difficult words can be
found in the glossary on pages 30 and 31.*

The INSIDE & OUT GUIDE to
YOUR BODY

STEVE PARKER

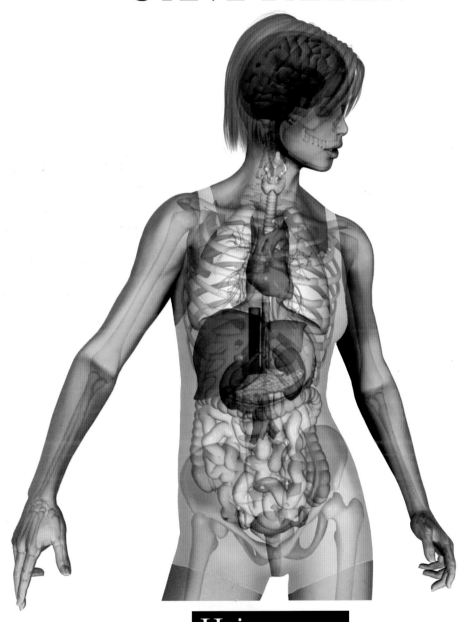

Heinemann
LIBRARY

CONTENTS

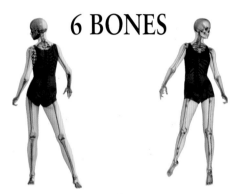

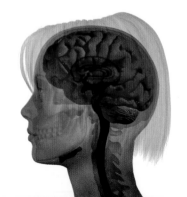
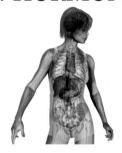
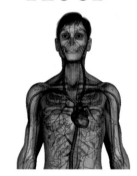
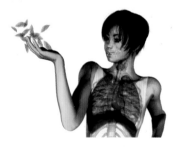
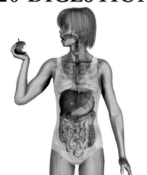

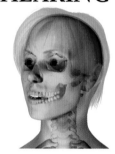

INTRODUCTION

WELCOME TO THE MOST STUDIED OBJECT IN THE history of the world – you. Perhaps not exactly yourself, but the human body. Nothing else has been looked at so often and in such detail, using all kinds of tools – from saws and scalpels to microscopes and scanners. As we turn the body inside out, to reveal more about its parts and how they work, we can also find out how to keep our own bodies healthy.

BONES

DIVIDE YOUR BODY WEIGHT BY SEVEN, AND THAT'S HOW much your bones weigh. Together, all of the 206 bones are known as the skeleton. They form a firm framework at the centre of the body, which is strong yet light, and moveable too. The skeleton supports the floppy parts draped around it, like blood vessels, nerves, and guts.

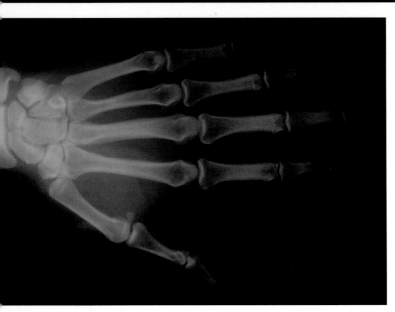

X-RAYS
The beam of an X-ray passes through soft body parts, like blood and nerves. X-rays cannot pass through hard materials, such as bones, which show up as white shapes.

Bones have many roles. Besides holding up the body, they also work as levers as muscles pull bones to cause movement. Bones provide protection. A strong, domed skull guards the delicate brain. The rib cage shields our heart and lungs. The spine is the long chain of bones that runs down our backs. It provides armour for the body's main nerve, the **spinal cord**. Bones also store minerals, such as calcium. When supplies are low, the body takes the calcium from bones. Then, the bones weaken, but they soon strengthen again with more calcium from food.

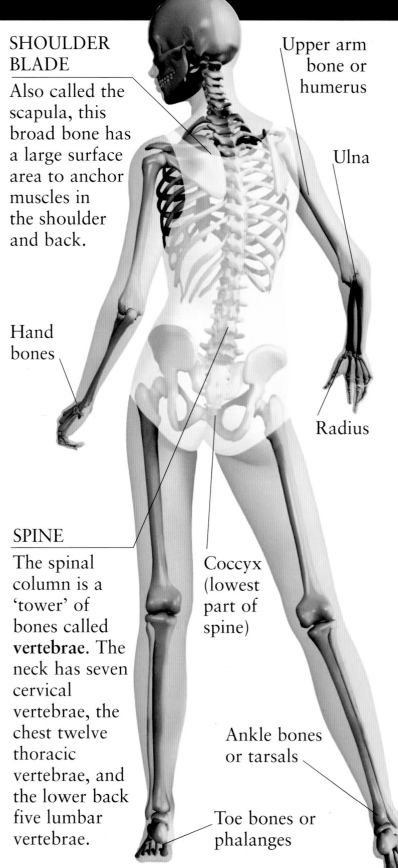

SHOULDER BLADE
Also called the scapula, this broad bone has a large surface area to anchor muscles in the shoulder and back.

Upper arm bone or humerus

Ulna

Hand bones

Radius

SPINE
The spinal column is a 'tower' of bones called **vertebrae**. The neck has seven cervical vertebrae, the chest twelve thoracic vertebrae, and the lower back five lumbar vertebrae.

Coccyx (lowest part of spine)

Ankle bones or tarsals

Toe bones or phalanges

We have an endoskeleton – one on the inside, with muscles around it. Insects like beetles have an outer casing, or exoskeleton, with muscles inside it.

Collar bone or clavicle

Breast bone or sternum

SKULL

Eight bones are fused together to form the upper domed part, called the cranium. There are fourteen bones in the face.

Solid or compact bone

Spongy or cancellous bone

RIBS

There are twelve pairs of ribs. The two lowermost pairs 'float' and do not join to the breast bone.

PELVIC BONE

Also called the hip bone, this widest body part anchors the thigh muscles. It is made of six bones joined firmly together.

Head of bone

Bone **marrow**

Shaft of bone

Sacrum (lower spine)

Thigh bone or femur

Kneecap or patella

Calf bone or fibula

Shin bone or tibia

Heel bone or calcaneus

Foot bones or metatarsals

INSIDE INFO: BONE

*The outer layer of solid bone is very hard and strong. Under it is a honeycomb-like layer to save weight. In the middle of some bones is soft, jelly-like marrow. This makes new microscopic red and white blood **cells** (below), three million per second, to replace those that wear out and die naturally.*

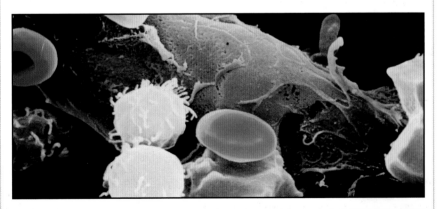

MUSCLES

EVERY MOVEMENT THE BODY MAKES IS POWERED BY muscles – more than 640 of them. In most people the muscle system forms about two-fifths of the body's weight, and has three main layers. These are superficial muscles just under the skin, intermediate muscles beneath them, and deep muscles which are innermost, next to the bones.

MORE MUSCLE OR MORE MUSCLES?
People with 'lots of muscles' have the same number as anyone else. But the individual muscles are bigger, with more fibres.

Even when sitting perfectly still, you constantly use muscles. Behind each eye, six small ribbon-like muscles cause the eyeball to swivel as you look around. Each blink is a contraction of your eyelid muscles. Typical muscles are long and slim. They taper at each end and are attached, by a strong, rope-like **tendon**, to a bone. Most body movements use dozens of muscles in teams. As they work together, each muscle pulls the bone in a slightly different direction, or steadies it, to make the movement firm, controlled, and precise. Meanwhile other muscles relax and are stretched.

NECK MUSCLES
The splenius capitus twists the head to look sideways.

Triceps brachii

TRAPEZIUS
This triangular muscle steadies and moves the shoulder blade.

Hamstrings

GLUTEUS MAXIMUS
The body's biggest muscle, forming the buttock, pulls the thigh bone back to walk, run, and jump.

GASTROCNEMIUS
This muscle makes the calf bulge as it pulls the heel up to tilt the foot and stand on tip-toe.

Achilles tendon

THE SMALLEST MUSCLE IS THE STAPEDIUS, THE SIZE OF THIS LETTER 'i'. IT PROTECTS THE INNER EAR FROM NOISES THAT ARE TOO LOUD.

The cheetah is the world's fastest runner, at 100 km/h. Yet it is lean and slim rather than stocky and muscular. Much of its speed is due to its long legs and bendy spine.

Extensor digitorum straightens fingers

Flexor carpi radialis

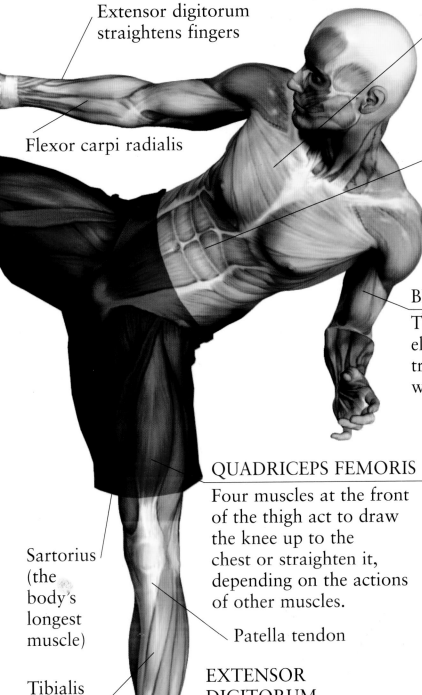

PECTORALIS MAJOR

The broad 'pecs' muscle joins to three bones. It can pull the shoulder forwards, thrust it back, or shrug it, depending which parts of it contract.

RECTUS ABDOMINIS

The 'six-pack' muscles help the body to bend forwards. If they tense at the same time as the back muscles tense, they make the belly (front abdomen) stiff and hard.

BICEPS BRACHII

This muscle bends the arm at the elbow. Its opposing partner is the triceps brachii (see opposite), which straightens the elbow.

QUADRICEPS FEMORIS

Four muscles at the front of the thigh act to draw the knee up to the chest or straighten it, depending on the actions of other muscles.

Patella tendon

EXTENSOR DIGITORUM LONGUS

This is one of the muscles that bends up the foot at the ankle and curls the toes.

Sartorius (the body's longest muscle)

Tibialis anterior

Extensor tendons to toes

INSIDE INFO: MUSCLE

A muscle contains tiny blood vessels and bundles, or fascicles, of muscle fibres (myofibres), each as thin as a hair. In turn, a single fibre contains muscle fibrils (myofibrils).

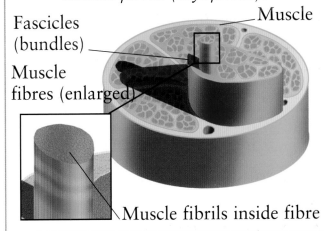

Fascicles (bundles)

Muscle

Muscle fibres (enlarged)

Muscle fibrils inside fibre

FLEXIBILITY

THE BODY'S 200-PLUS JOINTS OUT-PERFORM those of any machine. If looked after, they can work smoothly and silently for well over fifty years. They make their own 'oil' for lubrication. They also self-adjust for different conditions. And they can mend themselves after small problems such as minor sprains and injuries.

SUPPLE BODY
Use joints often (and with care) and they will stay flexible, allowing a full range of movement without stiffness or pain.

BALL AND SOCKET JOINT

The ball-shaped top of the thigh bone fits into a bowl-like socket in the hip bone, to allow movement in all directions as well as twisting, or rotation. The shoulder is similar but has a shallower socket.

A joint is where two or more bones meet. The amount of movement that it allows, and its strength and stability, depend partly on the shapes of bone ends and how they fit together. Also important are the muscles around the joint, which can both move and stabilize it. And there are slightly stretchy, belt-like ligaments which run from one bone around the joint to the other bone. These work like safety straps to stop the bones being wrenched too far. In general, the more movement in a joint, the less strength it has.

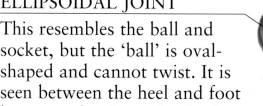

ELLIPSOIDAL JOINT

This resembles the ball and socket, but the 'ball' is oval-shaped and cannot twist. It is seen between the heel and foot bones, and wrist and palm bones.

A CAR ENGINE NEEDS LITRES OF OIL. THE KNEE JOINT HAS JUST A FEW DROPS OF OILY SYNOVIAL FLUID TO KEEP IT MOVING SMOOTHLY.

Cats are famous for their lithe bendiness. Their flexible joints combine with precise muscle control to move the bones accurately and keep them steady.

PIVOT JOINT

The topmost two bones of the spine are the ring-like atlas, and the axis, which has a peg-shaped part that sticks out. The pivot joint between them lets the skull twist and look to the right and left.

SADDLE JOINT

This joint allows two U-shaped bone ends to sit at right angles and slide past each other. It allows a great deal of flexibility back and forth as well as rotation. A saddle joint can be found where the base of your thumb meets your wrist.

PLANE JOINT

Several of the eight carpals (wrist bones) have almost flat sides or faces. They can slide across or glide past each other.

HINGE JOINT

The hinge joint in the knee is strong but limited. It allows the lower leg to move forwards and backwards only.

INSIDE INFO: JOINT

*The ends of bones are covered with shiny, smooth **cartilage** (gristle). Cartilage allows bones to slide past each other easily without wearing away. A tough capsule surrounds the joint. Its lining makes natural 'oil' called synovial fluid.*

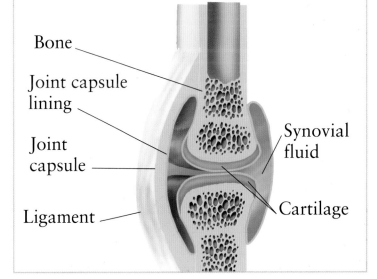

Bone

Joint capsule lining

Joint capsule

Ligament

Synovial fluid

Cartilage

11

BRAIN & NERVES

WE MAY SAY THAT WE FEEL emotions like love in our 'heart'. But emotions and feelings – as well as thoughts, memories, ideas and control of body systems – all happen in a soft, wrinkled, greyish-pink lump that fills the top half of the head.

The brain is not just the place for our thoughts, memories, and awareness of the world around us. It also carries out automatic processes that we rarely think about, such as breathing, heartbeat, and digestion. Each of these actions happens as tiny pulses of electricity, known as nerve signals. They pass among the brain's 100 billion microscopic nerve cells, or neurons, every split second. Nerves are bundles of hair-like nerve fibres. Sensory nerves carry signals from the eyes, ears, and other senses to the brain. Motor nerves take signals from the brain to the muscles.

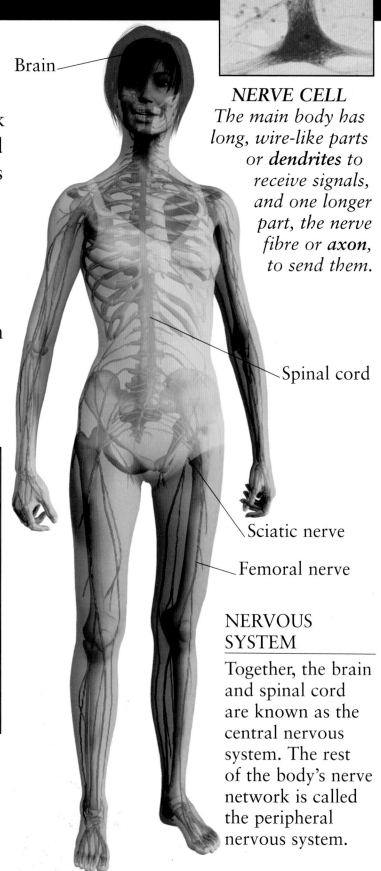

Brain

Spinal cord

Sciatic nerve

Femoral nerve

NERVE CELL
*The main body has long, wire-like parts or **dendrites** to receive signals, and one longer part, the nerve fibre or **axon**, to send them.*

NERVOUS SYSTEM

Together, the brain and spinal cord are known as the central nervous system. The rest of the body's nerve network is called the peripheral nervous system.

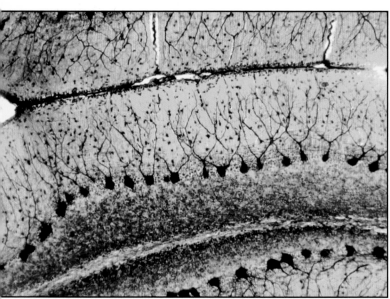

INSIDE INFO: CORTEX
*The **cortex** is the outer layer of the brain (see opposite). Its billions of nerve cells – shown here as dark blobs – have trillions of spider-like connections carrying nerve signals.*

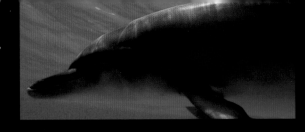

CEREBRAL CORTEX

The main upper brain is the **cerebrum**. Its outer layer is the cerebral cortex, where most thinking processes happen. It's as big as a pillowcase and 5 mm thick.

Pituitary **gland** (see next page)

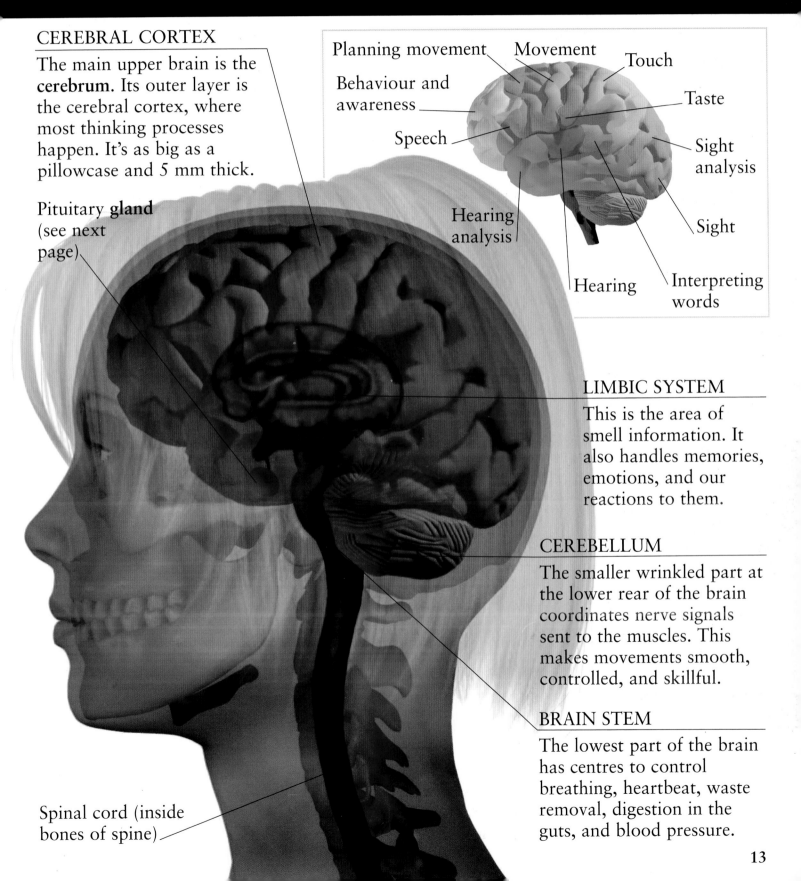

Planning movement
Movement
Touch
Behaviour and awareness
Taste
Speech
Sight analysis
Hearing analysis
Sight
Hearing
Interpreting words

LIMBIC SYSTEM

This is the area of smell information. It also handles memories, emotions, and our reactions to them.

CEREBELLUM

The smaller wrinkled part at the lower rear of the brain coordinates nerve signals sent to the muscles. This makes movements smooth, controlled, and skillful.

BRAIN STEM

The lowest part of the brain has centres to control breathing, heartbeat, waste removal, digestion in the guts, and blood pressure.

Spinal cord (inside bones of spine)

13

HORMONES

THE BRAIN CONTROLS MANY PROCESSES IN the body, such as heartbeat and muscle movements. But there is another control system, working mainly at a slower speed, over minutes, days, and even years. It uses chemical substances that travel in the blood to affect how the body works. These chemicals are called hormones.

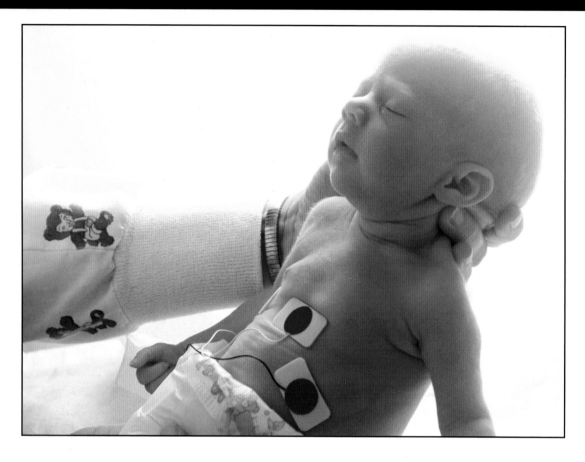

INSIDE INFO:
GROWING UP
One of the slowest processes under hormone control is growth. The tiny pituitary gland (see page 13) is located under the brain. It produces a hormone that causes body parts to grow. It helps bones to change shape and harden with age, as well as allowing muscles to develop.

Over a dozen body parts make hormones. Each one is called an endocrine gland and together these glands make up the endocrine system. Hormones are specific. They target selected areas of the body to cause particular reactions. Adrenaline, for example, targets muscles. Released when we are stressed or excited, it causes our hearts to beat faster and increases blood flow to the muscles. Adrenaline works alongside the nervous system to alert the body and prepare it for action. It is made in the adrenal glands, located on top of the kidneys. The hormone insulin, from the pancreas, controls the rate at which energy is used by the body. Increased levels of insulin in the blood slows down the rate at which the body uses energy. When the pancreas produces too little insulin, it causes the disorder diabetes.

SLEEP IS AFFECTED BY THE HORMONE MELATONIN. IT IS SECRETED AT NIGHT AND MADE IN A GLAND IN THE MIDDLE OF THE BRAIN CALLED THE PINEAL.

Growing into an adult, ready to mate with a partner and produce young is under the control of hormones – in animals as well as people.

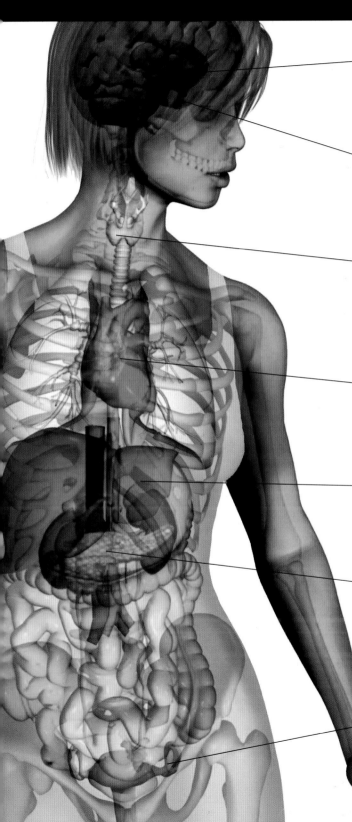

HYPOTHALAMUS

This gland in the lower front of the brain sends nerve signals and hormones to the pituitary, and links the nervous and hormonal systems.

PITUITARY GLAND

Smaller than a grape, the pituitary gland is the 'chief hormone gland'. Several of the hormones it secretes control other endocrine glands.

THYROID & PARATHYROID GLANDS

The thyroid makes two hormones that cause the body's cells to work faster and use more oxygen. A hormone from the parathyroid glands controls levels of calcium in the blood.

THYMUS GLAND

Located just in front of the heart, the thymus makes hormones that help white blood cells to attack and kill invading germs (see page 22).

ADRENAL GLANDS

Hormones released by the adrenal glands help to control waste removal, water balance, energy production, and how we respond to stress.

PANCREAS

The two hormones secreted by this leaf-shaped gland work together to control sugar levels in the blood. Insulin reduces the levels if they are high. When they are low, glucagon raises them.

OVARIES OR TESTES

In the female body, the ovaries produce two hormones, called oestrogen and progesterone, that control when egg cells are ready to be fertilized. In the male body, glands called testes make the testosterone. This hormone controls the growth of sperm cells.

HEART & BLOOD

EVERY MICROSCOPIC cell in the body needs a supply of oxygen and nutrients, and a waste-removal system. Flowing blood provides this service. Blood is kept on the move by a pump that is powerful, reliable, untiring, and self-adjusting – the heart.

The heart is a sack of special muscle, called cardiac muscle or myocardium. It contracts about once a second to squeeze blood into tubes, or vessels called **arteries**. These divide into microscopic tubes, called **capillaries**, which absorb food and oxygen before joining together to form vessels called **veins**. Veins return blood to the heart. The heart is a double pump. One side sends high-oxygen blood around the whole body, a process called systemic circulation. The other, known as pulmonary circulation, sends blood to and from the lungs, where it collects oxygen and gets rid of carbon dioxide.

ARTERIES & VEINS

Thick-walled arteries cope with high-pressure blood from the heart. Veins are wider with thin walls. Not all arteries carry bright red, high-oxygen blood. The pulmonary arteries to the lungs carry darker, low-oxygen blood. Pulmonary veins take high oxygen blood back to the heart.

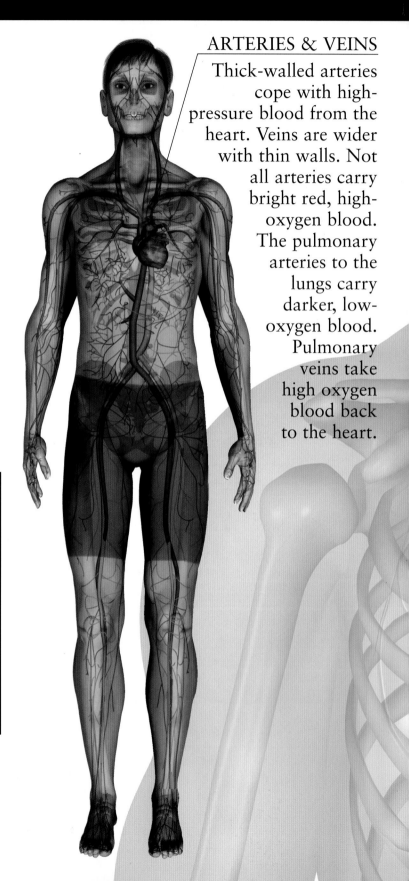

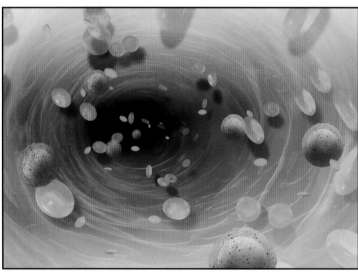

BLOOD CELLS
Blood contains three kinds of microscopic cells. Doughnut-like red cells carry oxygen. White cells change shape to fight and 'eat' invading germs. Platelets help blood to clot.

Many animals have red blood due to the colour of an oxygen-carrying, iron-containing substance, haemoglobin. A lobster has copper-based blue blood.

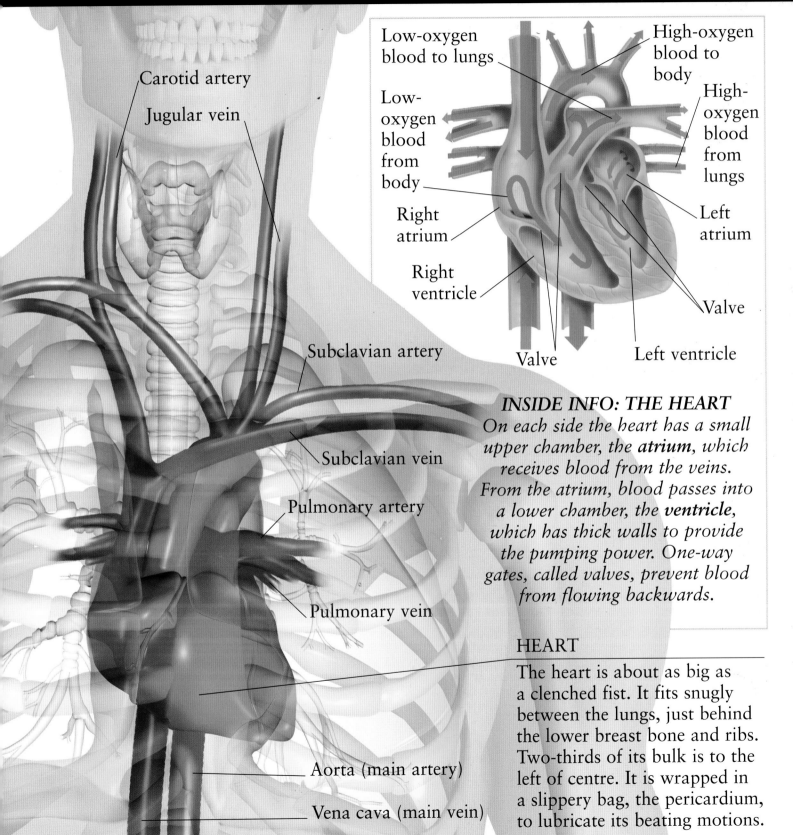

Carotid artery

Jugular vein

Subclavian artery

Subclavian vein

Pulmonary artery

Pulmonary vein

Aorta (main artery)

Vena cava (main vein)

Low-oxygen blood to lungs

High-oxygen blood to body

Low-oxygen blood from body

High-oxygen blood from lungs

Right atrium

Left atrium

Right ventricle

Valve

Valve

Left ventricle

INSIDE INFO: THE HEART

On each side the heart has a small upper chamber, the **atrium**, which receives blood from the veins. From the atrium, blood passes into a lower chamber, the **ventricle**, which has thick walls to provide the pumping power. One-way gates, called valves, prevent blood from flowing backwards.

HEART

The heart is about as big as a clenched fist. It fits snugly between the lungs, just behind the lower breast bone and ribs. Two-thirds of its bulk is to the left of centre. It is wrapped in a slippery bag, the pericardium, to lubricate its beating motions.

LUNGS & BREATHING

THE BODY'S most urgent need is not food, or water – it is oxygen. This unseen gas, with no smell or taste, makes up one-fifth of the air. The parts that take this oxygen into the body, for use by every one of its trillions of cells, make up the respiratory system.

To bring oxygen into the body, air is breathed in through the opening of the respiratory system – the nose and mouth. It passes down through the throat and windpipe, to the airways of the two lungs in the chest. The airways branch many times, becoming bronchi and then bronchioles, which are thinner than hairs. The bronchioles end in groups of microscopic 'bubbles' called **alveoli**. There are millions of alveoli in each lung. The alveoli walls are very thin and surrounded by the smallest blood vessels, called capillaries. Oxygen can easily pass from the air to the blood, and then spread around the body. The blood also contains the waste product carbon dioxide, which it has collected from the cells. This passes into the air in the alveoli and is breathed out.

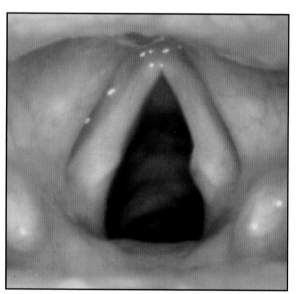 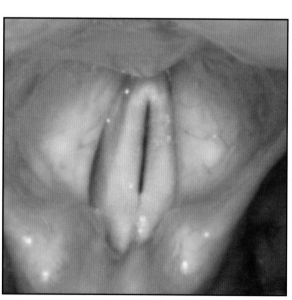

INSIDE INFO: VOCAL CORDS
*The two strap-like vocal cords are in the voicebox or **larynx**. Normally there is a wide gap between them (above left). For speech, they come close together and vibrate as air passes through the narrowed gap (above right).*

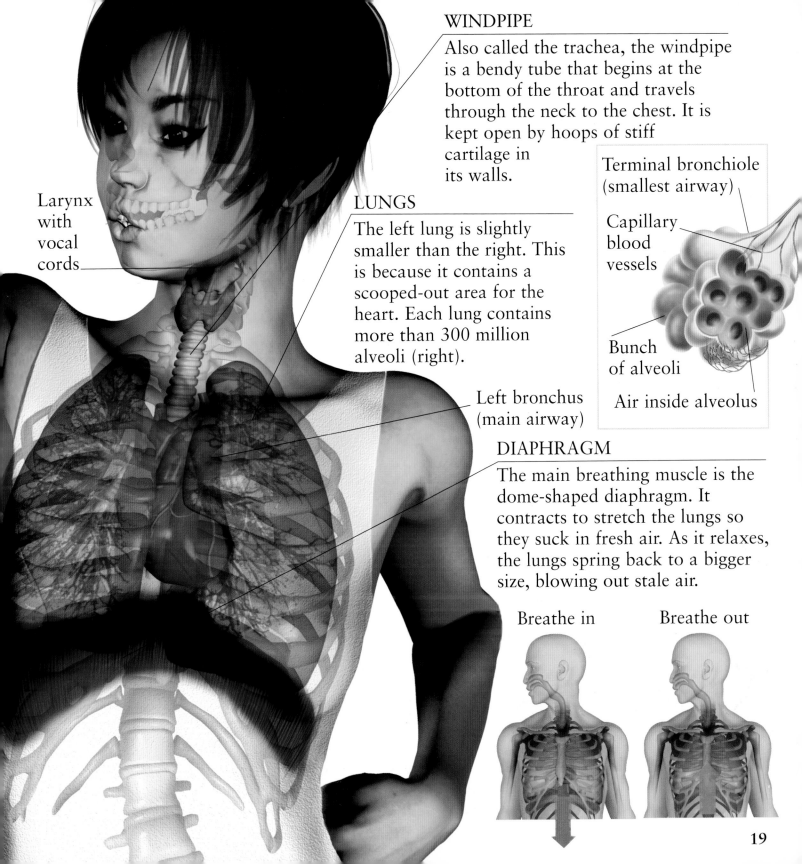

WINDPIPE

Also called the trachea, the windpipe is a bendy tube that begins at the bottom of the throat and travels through the neck to the chest. It is kept open by hoops of stiff cartilage in its walls.

Terminal bronchiole (smallest airway)

Capillary blood vessels

Bunch of alveoli

Air inside alveolus

LUNGS

The left lung is slightly smaller than the right. This is because it contains a scooped-out area for the heart. Each lung contains more than 300 million alveoli (right).

Larynx with vocal cords

Left bronchus (main airway)

DIAPHRAGM

The main breathing muscle is the dome-shaped diaphragm. It contracts to stretch the lungs so they suck in fresh air. As it relaxes, the lungs spring back to a bigger size, blowing out stale air.

Breathe in

Breathe out

19

The digestive tract is the long passageway that food takes as it travels through the body. It begins with the teeth, that grind down food, and includes the throat, the gullet (oesophagus), the stomach, the small intestine, which is six metres long, the large intestine, the rectum, where leftovers are stored, and finally the anus at the bottom end. The whole tract is about nine metres long. The tract breaks apart food physically, by squeezing and mashing. It attacks it chemically too, using substances called **enzymes** produced by the liver and pancreas. Together, these tubes and chemicals form the digestive system.

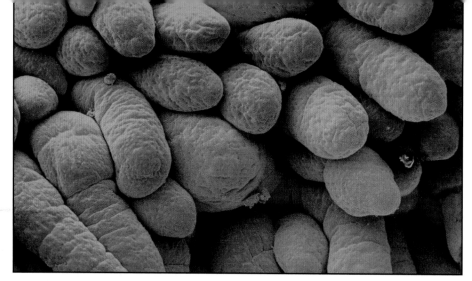

INSIDE INFO: VILLI

The small intestine is lined with finger-like structures called villi, each one is just one millimetre long. They absorb nutrients from digested food into the microscopic blood vessels inside them.

ENAMEL

The whitish outer layer of a tooth's upper part is the hardest material in the body.

DENTINE

Slightly softer than enamel, dentine absorbs knocks, jars and vibrations as we bite, crush, and crunch.

ROOT

Anchored into the jaw bone, the tooth's roots are a combination of fibre-like tissue and a 'living' cement.

GUM

The gingiva, or gum, seals the tooth's neck, between crown and roots.

DENTAL PULP

Tiny blood vessels nourish the tooth. Nerve endings can sense pressure and pain.

ROOT CANAL

The nerves and blood vessels pass into the tooth along this tunnel.

Animals like cow have a multi-part stomach. After eating, the cow 'coughs up' or regurgitates its food to munch again more thoroughly. This is called 'chewing the cud'.

MOUTH

The teeth bite off and mash up food. The tongue moves the lumps around so that they are all chewed to a pulp.

SALIVARY GLANDS

Six glands around the face produce saliva, which makes food slippery for swallowing.

GULLET

The muscular 'food pipe' pushes down swallowed food through the chest and into the stomach.

STOMACH

This is an expandable storage bag that writhes and squirms as it pours acids and enzymes on to the food.

KIDNEYS

These process the blood to remove waste and excess water.

Gall bladder

LIVER

The liver makes bile, a yellowish fluid stored in the gall bladder. It helps to digest fatty foods.

Pancreas

Appendix

SMALL INTESTINE

This is the main site for absorbing tiny bits of nutrients into the blood.

LARGE INTESTINE

Most of the water and useful minerals in leftover food are absorbed into the lining of the large intestine.

BLADDER

This is connected to the kidneys by the ureter. It stores urine, produced by the kidneys, ready to be passed out.

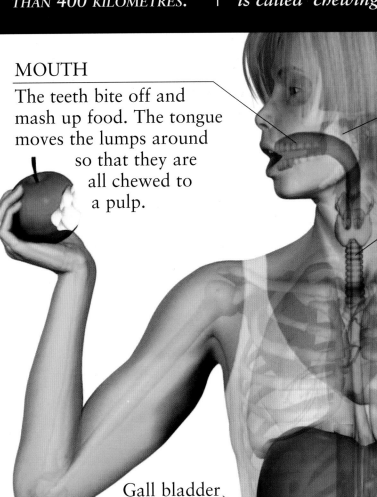

DEFENCES

EVERY SECOND, THE BODY IS UNDER ATTACK. Microscopic germs float unseen in the air and land on us, our food and our drinks. Small injuries happen as part of daily wear and tear. But the body has several lines of defence, from tough skin on the outside to white blood cells deep within.

Skin is the first line of defence. If it is cut or wounded, blood goes sticky and forms a clot. This creates a barrier that keeps out germs and prevents other fluids from leaking away. Another body fluid vital for defence is lymph. Lymph is the excess liquid that has passed from capillaries into tissues. Travelling down lymph vessels, it oozes into lymph nodes – these are the 'glands' which swell during illness – where it is filtered to check for disease. White blood cells form the basis of the **immune system**. They travel around the body, in blood and lymph, killing invaders such as viruses and germs.

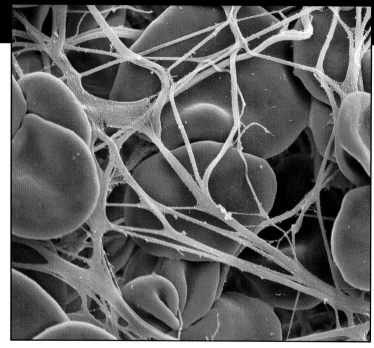

CLOTTING BLOOD
Damage to the skin, or an area inside the blood vessel causes blood to clot. A substance known as fibrin forms a sticky net that traps millions of platelets and red blood cells. This forms a sticky lump, the clot.

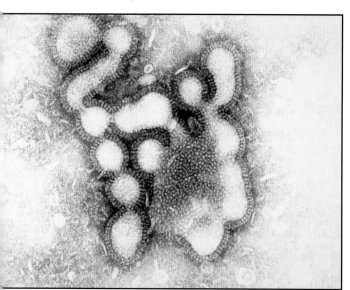

INFLUENZA ('FLU) VIRUS
Viruses are the smallest germs. Bacteria are bigger but still much tinier than the body's own cells.

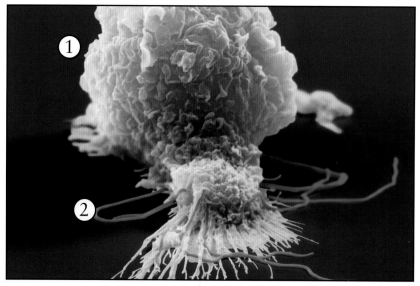

EATING THE INVADERS
The frilly white blood cells (1) called macrophages flow around and engulf germs such as these bacteria (2). The name macrophage means 'big eater'.

IN AN AVERAGE LIFETIME THE IMMUNE SYSTEM MAKES 100 BILLION BILLION ANTIBODIES. THEY FLOAT IN BLOOD AND LYMPH, ATTACKING GERMS.

Sharks rarely seem ill. Studying their immune system of white cells, antibodies, and other substances may help medical progress.

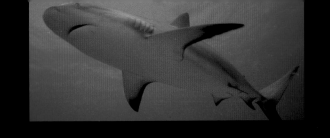

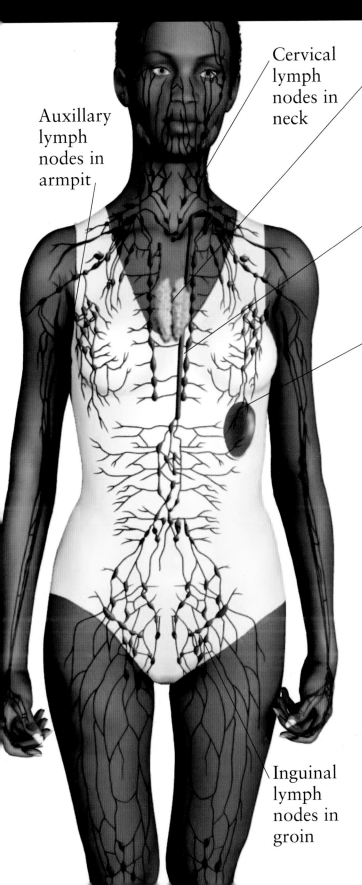

Cervical lymph nodes in neck

Auxillary lymph nodes in armpit

Inguinal lymph nodes in groin

THYMUS

The thymus is a gland that releases hormones that develop your immune system. It also 'trains' white blood cells called lymphocytes to become T-cells. These stick to germs and disable or kill them.

LYMPHATIC VESSELS AND DUCTS

Smaller vessels collect lymph, which flows through lymph nodes and finally into two main tubes, or ducts. These join to blood vessels near the heart, where lymph merges with blood.

SPLEEN

The spleen stores red blood cells and multiplying white blood cells. It also filters unwanted bits and pieces from blood.

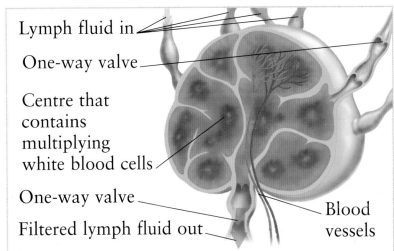

Lymph fluid in

One-way valve

Centre that contains multiplying white blood cells

One-way valve

Filtered lymph fluid out

Blood vessels

INSIDE INFO: LYMPH NODE
Lymph nodes remove debris and kill germs. Lymph fluid flows in along several small vessels and out through one larger one. Nodes vary from as small as rice grains to larger than grapes. During an infection they swell with extra lymph fluid, white cells and dead germs, and can be as big as tennis balls.

SEEING & HEARING

OUR SENSES ARE designed to detect what is happening around, on and inside the body, and send nerve signals to the brain. For many people the most important senses in daily life are sight and hearing.

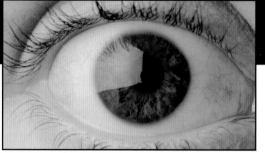

EYE COLOUR
*A coloured muscle ring, the iris, makes the pupil (hole) smaller in bright light, to protect the delicate **retina** within.*

Sense **organs** such as the eyes, ears, nose, tongue, and skin, are 'transducers'. This means that they gather information and change it into nerve signals for the brain. The eye's source of information is light rays. For the ears, it is sound waves. What we see, hear, smell, taste, and touch, does not become 'real' until the nerve signals from our sense organs reach our brain. Then the signals are sorted out and analyzed by different parts of the brain's upper surface, the cortex (see page 13). Only after this has happened, can we become aware in our mind of what our senses have detected.

HOW THE EYE WORKS

Light rays shine through the clear, domed cornea and into a hole, the pupil. The rays are bent by the lens to form a clear, sharp view on the retina lining at the back of the eyeball.

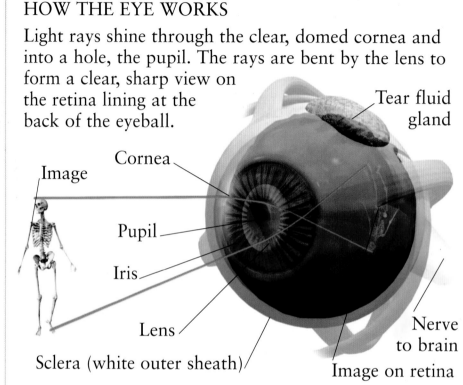

Image

Cornea

Tear fluid gland

Pupil

Iris

Lens

Sclera (white outer sheath)

Nerve to brain

Image on retina

HOW THE EAR WORKS

Sound waves hit the eardrum and make it vibrate. The vibrations pass along a row of three tiny bones. The last bone, the stirrup, transfers the vibrations into the snail-like **cochlea** which turns them into nerve signals.

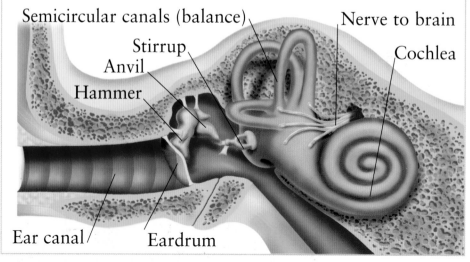

Semicircular canals (balance)

Stirrup

Anvil

Hammer

Nerve to brain

Cochlea

Ear canal

Eardrum

THE EYE'S RETINA HAS MORE THAN **120** MILLION LIGHT-SENSING CELLS, RODS AND CONES. BUT ONLY THE SIX MILLION CONES CAN SEE COLOURS.

Owls have huge eyes, filling almost half the head. They also have amazing hearing, although their ear openings are hidden under feathers.

EYE

Each eye is protected in a 'bowl' of skull bone, the eye socket or orbit. Every few seconds watery fluid from the tear gland under the outer eyelid is blinked over the eye's surface, the conjunctiva, to keep it moist and clean.

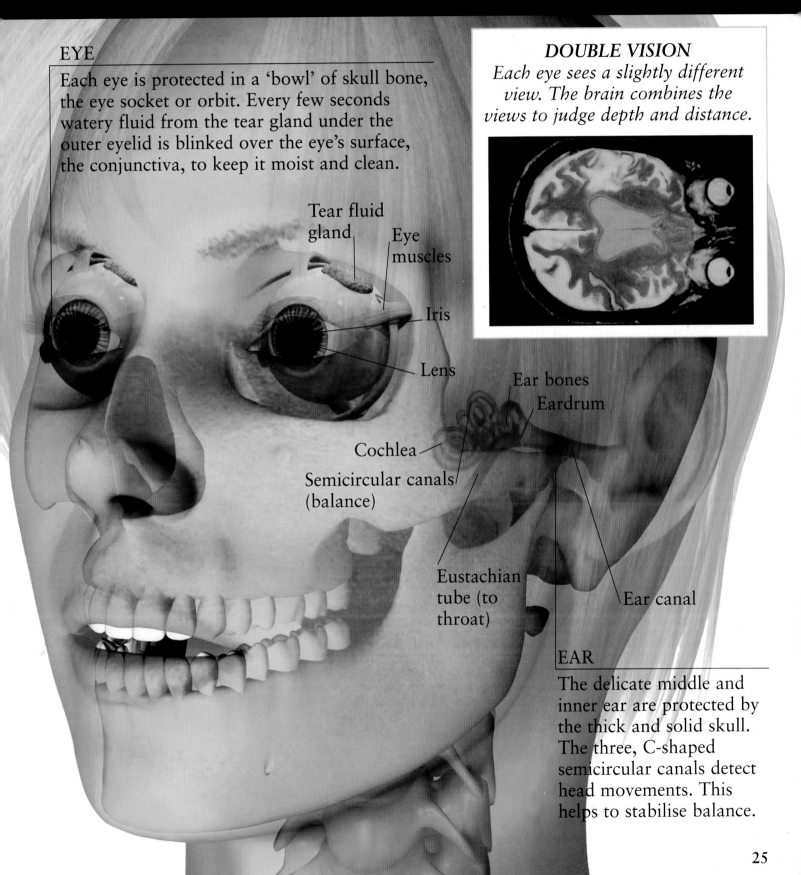

Tear fluid gland

Eye muscles

Iris

Lens

Ear bones

Eardrum

Cochlea

Semicircular canals (balance)

Eustachian tube (to throat)

Ear canal

DOUBLE VISION

Each eye sees a slightly different view. The brain combines the views to judge depth and distance.

EAR

The delicate middle and inner ear are protected by the thick and solid skull. The three, C-shaped semicircular canals detect head movements. This helps to stabilise balance.

TASTE & SMELL

If we try a strange new food, we usually take a sniff first, and test a tiny piece for flavour. The senses of smell and taste help us to check if food is bad or 'off' – and they also give the pleasure of a delicious meal.

Smell and taste work in similar ways. They are known as chemosenses because they work by picking up odour particles that float in the air, and flavour particles from food and drinks. These particles touch tiny hairs, called cilia, which stick out from hair cells. If one of these minute particles fits into a slot on the cilia hair, the hair cell sends nerve signals to the brain. These signals are read by the brain as different types of taste and odour. Hair cells that detect smells live in your nose. For taste, they sit in buds mainly on the upper surface of your tongue.

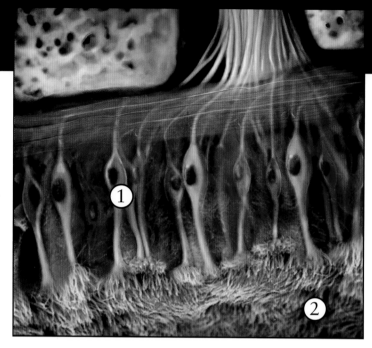

IN THE ROOF OF THE NOSE
More than 20 million hair cells, called **olfactory** *cells (1), have tufts of cilia (2) hanging from them. Each smell has a certain shape of scent particle that fits into similar-shaped 'landing sites' on the cilia.*

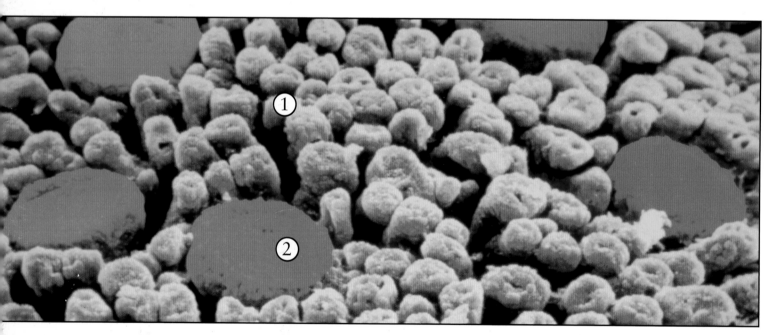

ON THE SURFACE OF THE TONGUE
The tongue is covered by tiny lumps of different shapes called papillae. Some are long and thin, like fingers (1), others are shorter and wider (2). On the sides of these lumps, and between them, are about 10,000 small taste buds that detect flavours.

TASTE BUDS GRADUALLY DIE WITH AGE. AN OLDER PERSON MAY HAVE 5,000 OR FEWER, AND SAY THAT FOODS ARE 'NOT AS TASTY AS THEY USED TO BE'.

we have about 20 million olfactory hair 'smell cells'. A dog has ten times as many and senses smells that are so faint we would never notice them.

SMELL

The roof of the nose is covered with olfactory hair cells. Nerves pass from these cells, through the skull bone, to an area called the olfactory bulb. This sorts and processes the nerve signals before they go to the brain.

Olfactory bulb

Olfactory tract into brain

Olfactory nerves

Olfactory hair cells

Nerves from tongue to brain

TASTE

Tiny nerves from thousands of taste buds come together to form branches of two main nerves in the head. These convey the signals to the brain.

TASTE MAP

It is thought that tastes are made from different proportions of the five basic flavours. These are sweet, salty, sour, bitter, and umami (meaty). They are detected in particular areas of the tongue.

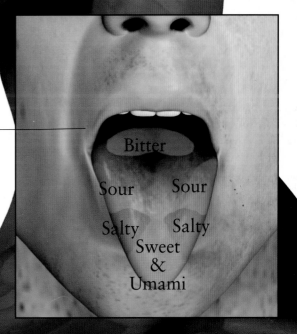

Bitter

Sour   Sour

Salty   Salty

Sweet & Umami

SKIN, HAIR, & NAILS

THE BODY HAS A new outer surface every month. The upper layer of the skin is worn away during this time, but it replaces itself continuously from below. Hairs and nails are made from a similar substance to outer skin, called keratin, and they also grow constantly.

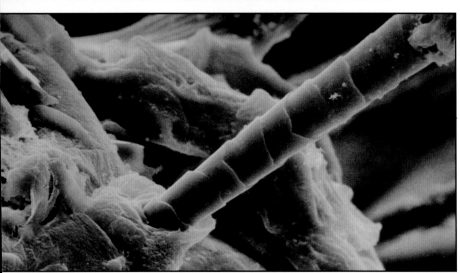

SCALY HAIR

A hair's shaft is coated with 'scales' made of flattened, dead hair cells. A typical head hair grows about 3 mm in one week. Darker, coarse hair lengthens faster than lighter, finer hair.

Skin is the body's biggest organ. It weighs up to four kilograms. If it were flattened out it would cover nearly two square metres – twice the size of a beach towel. The outer layer of skin, called the epidermis, contains a layer of cells that multiply very quickly. Gradually, they flatten out, fill with a keratin (the same substance that hair and nails are made of) and die. The dead cells are pushed up to the surface by more new cells from below, where they are worn away before flaking off. Under the epidermis is the dermis. This houses nerve endings for touch, sweat glands, hair roots, and sebaceous glands. Sebaceous glands make a natural oil, known as sebum, that keeps skin stretchy.

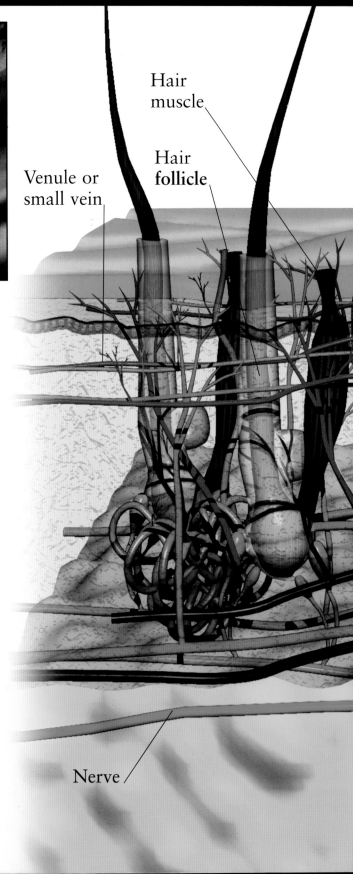

Hair muscle

Hair **follicle**

Venule or small vein

Nerve

A HEAD HAIR MAY GROW FOR UP TO FIVE YEARS BEFORE FALLING OUT AND BEING REPLACED. AN EYELASH HAIR DOES THIS IN ONLY TEN WEEKS.

Each hair has a tiny muscle that pulls it upright, which causes a 'goose-bump'. This effect is much clearer in animals who 'fluff up' their fur.

Sweat droplet oozing from a sweat pore

Arteriole or small artery

Sebaceous gland

HAIRS

There are about 100,000 hairs on the head, and more than 10 million much smaller, thinner hairs over the whole body. Hairs grow from tiny pits called hair follicles.

EPIDERMIS

Skin's colour comes from a substance called melanin, which is made in the base of the epidermis. The amount of melanin made is inherited from our parents.

NERVE ENDINGS

Different shaped nerve endings (shown in green) sense different features of touch. They look like tiny branches or rounded buds.

DERMIS

The lower layer of skin is thicker than the epidermis, except in areas of greater wear and pressure, like the soles of the feet.

BLOOD VESSELS

If the body is hot, blood vessels widen so that heat can pass from the blood into the air. This makes the skin look red.

SWEAT GLAND

About three million sweat glands (shown in purple) lose sweat even if the body is resting. A hot, active person can lose a litre per hour.

SUBCUTANEOUS FAT

This layer helps to absorb knocks and blows. It also works as insulation to keep core body temperature steady in extreme cold or heat.

GLOSSARY

alveoli
The millions of microscopic 'bubbles' in the lungs, where oxygen passes from air into the capillary blood vessels around, and carbon dioxide passes in the opposite direction.

antibodies
Substances produced by white blood cells that help the body fight disease.

artery
A large blood vessel (tube) that carries blood away from the heart.

atrium
One of the two small, thin-walled upper chambers of the heart.

axon
A long, thin, wire-like part of a nerve cell, also called a nerve fibre, which passes nerve signals to other nerve cells, or to muscles, or glands.

capillary
The smallest type of blood vessel that allows oxygen and nutrients to pass out from the blood and waste products to move into the blood.

cartilage
A smooth, bendy substance that shapes body parts like the nose and also covers the ends of bones in a joint.

cell
A tiny 'building block' of the body. There are billions of cells, of different shapes and sizes, like skin cells, nerve cells, and bone cells.

cerebrum
The main dome-shaped, wrinkled upper part of the brain, which forms over three-quarters of its total volume.

cochlea
A part of the ear, found deep inside, shaped like a snail. It changes the vibration movements of sounds into nerve signals.

cortex
The thin grey covering of the brain's cerebrum (see above). This area enables us to understand our thoughts, surroundings, and actions.

dendrite
Short, wire-like part of a nerve cell that gathers nerve signals.

enzyme
Chemical that changes complex nutrients into simple ones.

follicle
The tiny pit in the dermis (lower layer of skin) from which a hair grows.

gland
A body part that makes and releases a product, such as a sweat gland, which makes sweat, or a salivary gland, which produces saliva (spit).

hormone
A natural body chemical that travels in the blood and controls the workings of certain body parts known as its targets.

immune system
Parts of the body which defend against germs, diseases, and illness.

larynx
The voice-box at the top of the windpipe (trachea) in the neck, which makes the sounds of the voice.

marrow
A soft, jelly-like substance inside certain bones, which stores energy as fat, and in some bones makes new cells for the blood.

nutrients
Substances taken in by the body that provide energy for growth or repair.

olfactory
To do with the nose and the sense of smell.

organ
A main part of the body, such as the brain, heart, stomach, or skin.

retina
The light-detecting layer on the inside of the back of the eyeball, which changes patterns of light rays into nerve signals.

spinal cord
The main nerve from the base of the brain, which runs down inside the spine (backbone) and has nerve branches to all body parts.

tendon
The strong, rope-like, tapering end of a muscle, which joins firmly to a bone.

vein
A large blood vessel (tube) carrying blood towards the heart.

ventricle
One of the two large, thick-walled lower chambers of the heart, which pumps blood out into the arteries.

vertebra
One of the individual bones making up the spinal column (called the spine or backbone).

INDEX